Intersections:
Where Faith and Life Meet

A Cumberland Presbyterian
Adult Resource
Volume 17, Lent, Easter, Pentecost, Year 3

Discipleship Ministry Team
Ministry Council
Cumberland Presbyterian Church

8207 Traditional Place
Cordova, Tennessee 38016

First Edition 2017

Published by The Discipleship Ministry Team
General Assembly Ministry Council of the Cumberland Presbyterian Church
Cordova, Tennessee

ISBN-13: 978-1-945929-06-9
ISBN-10: 1-945929-06-5

We want to hear from you.
Please send your comments about this curriculum to
the Discipleship Ministry Team at chm@cumberland.org.

OUR UNITED OUTREACH
Made Possible In Part By Your Tithe To Our United Outreach

Table of Contents

Editor: Cindy Martin

To order, call 901-276-4572, x 252 or e-mail resources@cumberland.org.

What Keeps Us From Yelling?

Scripture for lesson: Mark 10:46-52

Written by Stephen Shelton

When have you, or someone close to you, screamed in excitement, fear, or desperation? On the other hand, what memory do you have of an extremely uncomfortable silence? Which is easier for you to hear?

For my daughter Catherine's 5th birthday, we took a family vacation to Walt Disney World. We visited every park, saw almost every character, and rode nearly every ride—that a five-year-old could ride. At the midpoint of our time in the Orlando area, we left Disney World and went to Sea World. After watching the dolphin and sea lion shows and a few other things, we took a break to rest at a massive, elevated playground. This playground was the size of a football field and only had two entrances/exits. Inside the playground was a spaghetti pile of tunnels, cargo nets, slides, and platforms. After no more than five minutes of playing on the behemoth, I lost track of which tunnel my daughter was in.

My eyes squinted in the bright sunlight as I searched again and again, looking for any sign of Catherine's bright orange pants or blue bow. I ran below the structure to position myself between the two entrances, hoping to catch her when she tired and got off. I watched, I waited, I paced, I walked, I climbed briefly into the lowest level, and I climbed back down. Through all of the walking and pacing and climbing, I worried. After what seemed like an hour (but was, in reality, about 10 minutes) I finally caught a brief glimpse of a blue bow followed by bright orange pants coming out of a third level tunnel. In relief and excitement, I screamed at the top of my lungs, "CATHERINE!" Probably a hundred sets of eyes (including my daughter's) immediately turned to find out who the crazy dad was below the playground.

Normally I would not have screamed for my daughter, especially in front of a group of complete strangers, but I was extremely concerned about her. My embarrassment about yelling in front of strangers was overcome by my need to make sure my daughter was safe.

Prep for the Journey

As this story unfolds, Jesus and his disciples were leaving Jericho. Mark's references to travel and location begin to move Jesus intentionally through neighboring cities with an ultimate destination of Jerusalem. The political and religious environments in Judah were becoming increasingly volatile, especially where Jesus was concerned. His disciples tried to convince Jesus not to make the journey to Jerusalem for the Passover celebration, but Jesus refused.

Looking back at their recent travels, we see the disciples beginning to covet their time with Jesus and a growing dislike of sharing him with others. Some good examples are when the disciples were worried about others using Jesus' name (Mark 9:38), trying to get rid of children (10:13), and desiring to be close to him eternally (Mark 10: 37). Whether we like their reasoning or not, the disciples closest to Jesus showed their desire to protect Jesus and keep him at a greater distance from others.

Jesus was becoming increasingly focused on what he knew awaited him in Jerusalem. He told his disciples three different times in three consecutive chapters that he would die and be resurrected. Chapter 10 contains one of these references. With these and other subtle changes taking place in Jesus' ministry (fewer healings and more teachings as compared to the first half of Mark) and travels, it would seem to me that the disciples would be a little uneasy about someone yelling at their teacher, which happened on their way out of Jericho.

On the Road

The disciples likely would have been sensitive to Jesus' changing mood and his reduction in action as well as his emphasis on thought and introspection. As we look at where this event takes place in Mark's time line of Jesus' ministry, the verse that immediately follows the scripture for this lesson has Jesus triumphantly arriving in Jerusalem, which began his final week of life on earth.

Read Mark 10:46.

They came to Jericho. As he and his disciples and a large crowd were leaving Jericho, Bartimaeus son of Timaeus, a blind beggar, was sitting by the roadside.

When have you tried to stop someone from continuing on a path that seemed to be fraught with danger? What happened?

With whom do you covet spending time? How have you found extra time with this person?

What is your first reaction when a stranger calls out to you? Why?

How aware are you of a leader's change in mood? How would you be better served if you were more aware?

We don't know how long Bartimaeus had been blind or what caused his blindness. Neither of those details matters. Sitting in the street for the last years and months, he had undoubtedly heard countless rumors of a traveling teacher, healer, and Messiah: Jesus. We can imagine his eagerness to meet this Jesus.

Read Mark 10:47-48.

When he heard that it was Jesus of Nazareth, he began to shout out and say, "Jesus, Son of David, have mercy on me!" 48 Many sternly ordered him to be quiet, but he cried out even more loudly, "Son of David, have mercy on me!"

On this day in particular, Bartimaeus heard the excited whispers on the street that Jesus was passing through his city, Jericho. Not being able to see who was on his street or what crowd belonged to what leader or teacher, Bartimaeus likely was yelling all day at any gathering of voices who walked past, hoping with all his soul that Jesus was among them.

It's likely that others who also spent a great deal of time on his street (shop owners, other beggars, guards, etc.) would have grown tired of his excitement and yelling during the day. So, between the disciples who were guarding Jesus' time and attention and the other people who were on the street with Bartimaeus, there aren't many who would have been very patient with his shouting.

The moment arrived for the blind beggar. The noise of the crowd was vast this time. This group seemed to be much larger than the others. The whispers of those around Bartimaeus started to include the name Jesus. He knew that it was time; it was, perhaps, his only chance at a full life. He began to yell with all of his strength, asking Jesus, "Son of David," to have mercy on him.

It doesn't take a biblical scholar to recognize the name of Israel's most beloved king. To attach Jesus' name to the lineage of David made him royalty. In Roman times, to call someone king like that would have meant arrest, at least, and death, at worst. Despite the protests of those around him, likely even including those of the disciples, he doubled down on his efforts and continued to yell.

Read Mark 10:49-52.

Jesus stood still and said, "Call him here." And they called the blind man, saying to him, "Take heart; get up, he is calling you." 50 So throwing off his cloak, he sprang up and came to Jesus. 51 Then Jesus said to him, "What do you want me to do for you?" The blind man said to him, "My teacher, let me see again." 52 Jesus said to him, "Go; your faith has made you well." Immediately he regained his sight and followed him on the way.

It is amazing how Jesus heard the voice of one man above all of the chatter of the large crowd that surrounded him. We can imagine that those people who had earlier ordered Bartimaeus to be quiet may have had to re-evaluate their opinion. If Jesus bothered to stop and talk with this beggar, he must not be all bad.

As soon as the beggar was told that Jesus was calling to him, he left his cloak and began to move toward Jesus. The mention of Bartimaeus leaving his cloak behind is very telling. He obviously responded to Jesus immediately, without thought about anything else. A man's cloak was considered a basic necessity. In fact, it was not to be loaned and creditors were forbidden to keep it overnight. The cloak was used as a covering at night. As a beggar, Bartimaeus would not have been able to replace his cloak easily, yet he didn't give it a second thought when Jesus beckoned.

Jesus immediately healed Bartimaeus, who joined the crowd that was following Jesus. We don't know any more about this man other than that he had enough faith to call out to Jesus.

Scenic Route

In ancient Israel, life for someone with a disability was not easy. A disability was thought to be a sign that within your family (especially your father or your father's father) was a significant sin for which you were being punished. People of that time thought that nothing was without cause; therefore, God's wrath had visited you with a disability for a reason, even if the reason was unknown. Because of this connection between a disability and sin, someone with a visible impairment was not allowed in the Temple, and was definitely not to approach the altar. (Read Leviticus 21:16-23 for more information on this law). Consequently, a person who had a disability could not participate in Temple worship, disconnecting him from the core of Jewish spiritual life.

Making things even worse for one with a disability was his or her inability to work. The person's family was responsible for providing a home, food, clothes and other basic necessities, which was generally a hardship. Begging was the only option for adding to the family's income. A disabled person usually found a spot where a lot of people would pass by and went there every day to ask for handouts. The more serious the disability, the greater the likelihood of getting handouts. In fact, there are records of disabled people being mutilated or disfigured further by their parents or by themselves so that their begging might be more successful.

Let us now consider Jesus. Jericho was only a short distance from Jerusalem, which means that it was one of Jesus' last stops before triumphantly entering Jerusalem. The dusty roads would have been crowded with pilgrims headed to the city to celebrate Passover. As Jesus and his disciples walked with the crowd, he undoubtedly was thinking about the events to come. Even with all this on his mind, Jesus took time out for Bartimaeus. What a patient and wonderful savior.

How do you respond when Jesus calls?

When have you called out to Jesus? How persistent were your pleas?

How do you respond to someone who deals with the challenges of a disability?

In what ways does your congregation welcome people who have disabilities? How accessible is your building? What adaptations could be made so that a person with limitations would find it easier to worship there?

Why do you think Jesus responded to Bartimaeus? How much did the beggar's desperation and determination influence Jesus? Would Jesus have noticed him and healed him without his cries and shouting?

Workers Ahead

How do you feel when someone approaches you to ask for a handout? How do you react?

To whom do you need to stop and speak?

How willing are you to form a relationship with people such as the blind beggar? Why?

What empowers and/or encourages you to call out to Christ?

Although the United States has social programs in place to provide care for those who have a disability, those programs fall woefully short in meeting all of the myriad of needs such people have. For instance, the monthly government stipend is not enough to pay for adequate housing in most areas. It certainly won't cover nutritious food or medications not allowed by Medicaid. Forget any of the extras such as clothing, haircuts, or dental care. As was true in Bible times, families often end up helping to support these individuals, or these people end up living on the streets.

We see people looking for handouts nearly everywhere these days. Some of them have a legitimate need—a disability, homelessness, a prison record, etc. We often think that a person who is homeless should just get a job. It isn't that easy. When a person is homeless, he or she doesn't have a permanent address, which is required for many job applications. He or she may not have a cell phone, so there is no way for a potential employer to contact him or her. Getting a shower and appropriate clothing for an interview can also be an issue. Even after a person has served his or her prison sentence, many employers are reluctant to hire him or her. All of these issues contribute to the number of people we see looking for handouts.

Unlike Bartimaeus, these people are crying out silently. Many of them don't feel as if they have a voice, as if anyone cares about them. We walk by them on the street, often averting our eyes. We donate to the church's food pantry or clothes closet and think we have done our part. But Jesus showed us what is most important: establishing a relationship with people. He stopped and talked to the blind beggar.

In the Rear View

The question that naturally comes to mind when encountering this story is, "What keeps us from yelling?" There's no end to the number of distractions and discouragements we can experience as believers and as disciples. Even though Jesus' disciples seemed to be hindered somewhat during these last days, Bartimaeus was anything but hindered. Through this man's faith and his courage to speak aloud the name and heritage of Jesus, we can see a wonderful example of what it means to shout the truth, even if it might be risky to do so.

As you close your time together, pray aloud this prayer in unison: Almighty and gracious God, there are days when we want to be quiet and anonymous and not intrude into the lives of others. There are also days when we see people in need of your love, your grace, your mercy, and we think about acting, about using our voices for you. Move within us through your Spirit, O God, and give us your voice and your words so that we speak truth in Love. Give us the desperation of Bartimaeus so that our words have passion. Amen.

Travel Log

Day 1:

As we begin this journey looking at the shouting stones of Jesus' last few days of earthly ministry, we will need to compare ourselves to our biblical counterparts who were also seeking discipleship in Jesus. Take some time to reflect quietly or journal your thoughts about the importance of using your voice in being a follower of Jesus, especially when others are not using their voices.

Day 2:

The disciples has begun to protect their time with Jesus, wanting to spend as much time with him as possible. How do you protect your time with Jesus? If you need to be more intentional about protecting this time, make some notes in the space below as to how you might accomplish that goal.

Day 3:

Whose voice have you tried to silence rather than help it to be heard? Why did you feel it needed to be silenced? How do you feel about your actions now? Journal your responses to the questions.

Day 4:

Why do you think Bartimaeus referred to Jesus as "Son of David"? What designation today would carry such a significant meaning for the average person? Jot down some ideas below.

Day 5:

Those who have disabilities may feel as isolated from the church as did the blind beggar. Whom do you know who struggles with a disability? How are you reaching out to this person? How might your group and/or congregation reach out more intentionally to people who have disabilities?

Day 6:

While the question of what keeps us from yelling is an important one to ask, it might also be worth asking yourself, "What would give me courage enough to yell?" or at least approach that person you think might need to hear your words. Make a list of people whom you think might need to hear your words. Then identify some ways of sharing your words with them.

Day 7:

   People in our society are craving relationships. They want to know that someone cares about them, which is especially true of young adults. How can you develop relationships with people of all ages? Make notes below and then follow through!

Speaking Out of Turn

Scripture for Lesson: Matthew 27:15-26

Written by Steven Shelton

What would cause you to speak out of turn? When have you done so? What happened?

When have you faced a disagreement, frustration, or difficult situation over which you had little to no power or influence? How did you react? How did you resolve the situation (or was it unresolved)?

I have a pastor friend who leads a medium-sized Baptist church in our community. He and I, as well as several other pastors, work together on community worship services and cooperative ministries. In a recent planning meeting, he shared this story, told here from his perspective:

"Janet has been a member of our church for a long time, but she recently became my 'thorn in the flesh,'—probably so God can teach me about the life of Paul. (laughter) What sparked her behavior change was our administration team's decision to dismiss our children's minister and seek out a new person for the position. Janet (the wife of one of our deacons) called my office to voice her displeasure after the meeting and told me that we absolutely should not act on that decision. I immediately dismissed her and her disparaging opinions because we needed to move on from our current situation. I informed her that while I appreciated her opinion, she didn't have a say in the situation because she was not on the administration team. Our conversation became so angry that I doubted I would ever see her in worship again. But the very next Sunday, she was sitting in her normal place on the second row. During the sermon, she crossed her arms and scowled, refusing to make eye contact with me the entire time I was speaking.

She continued this behavior the week before we let our children's minister go and continued it for three months after we actually dismissed the employee. Each Sunday, she voiced her silent protest by sitting in her seat, crossing her arms, and refusing to look at me. Come to find out, she was right. In the aftermath of letting our children's director go, we lost three families, all of which had young children. Our administration team wasn't prepared for that reaction to our decision. Sometimes I wonder if I should have listened to this woman who spoke out of turn."

Prep for the Journey

Rome conquered Jerusalem in 63 B.C., but used local people in leadership roles. Herod the Great was one such person. After his death in 4 B.C., his son Herod Antipas became ruler over Galilee. This Herod is the one Matthew mentioned in the story of Jesus' birth. He ruled for about eight years, at which time Rome sent Pontius Pilate to serve as governor of the region.

The Jewish people had an intense hatred for the Romans. They hated them for their domination as well as the influence they were having culturally. "Jewish Palestine had (in theory) been restored to a theocracy, meaning the law of God was also the law of the land. In reality it was an occupied country with little power of its own. Jewish leadership was in the hands of the high priest, whose power, although restricted to the Jewish world, extended into religious, political, and administrative realms" (*The Land and People Jesus Knew*, by J. Robert Teringo, © 1985, page 168).

The events covered in this lesson started with the arrest of Jesus in the garden, where he had gone to pray after celebrating the Passover with his disciples. While in the garden, a large crowd came, led by the chief priests and elders of the people. Judas Iscariot identified Jesus for the crowd by kissing him, which was a natural way for disciples to greet their teacher. Many people in the crowd had brought swords and clubs, fearing that Jesus would resist arrest.

Jesus was taken to the home of Caiaphas, the high priest, where Matthew tells us the entire council of religious leaders had gathered. However, holding such a meeting at night violated several Jewish laws, and definitely would not have been done during a festival time. They may have gathered "at night in the hope of gathering evidence against Jesus. They were unable to find witnesses whose testimony agreed on any point that would make a conviction possible…Thus it would have been quite impossible to convict Jesus in a Jewish court" (*The Interpreter's Bible, Vol. 7*, ©1951, page 586).

On the Road

Although those who wrote the Gospel accounts of that night were not present for the proceedings, we are told that the priestly council tried to get Jesus to admit to being the Messiah so that they could "accuse him to Pilate as a pretender to the Jewish throne" (ibid). Jesus

Where are people experiencing domination by foreign countries today? How would you compare that domination to what you know about the Romans in Jesus time?

If you had been in Jerusalem at this time, what would have caused you to agree or disagree with the council's claims regarding Jesus?

How do you feel when there is not sufficient evidence to convict someone whom you have decided is guilty?

When have you been lured into doing another person's dirty work? How did you feel when you realized what had happened?

When have you seen "crowd mentality" supersede rational actions? How can such a situation be handled so that it doesn't become violent?

When has advice come to you from an unexpected source? How did you react?

When have you given advice that was ignored? What happened? How did you react?

was taken before the Roman authorities in chains, accused of breaking non-Roman religious laws. Given that Pilate seemed to delight in provoking Jewish sensibilities at every turn, it seems odd that the Jewish officials turned to him. However, since they could not condemn Jesus to death, they wanted Pilate to do their dirty work.

Read Matthew 27:15-18.

Now at the festival the governor was accustomed to release a prisoner for the crowd, anyone whom they wanted. ¹⁶ *At that time they had a notorious prisoner, called Jesus Barabbas.* ¹⁷ *So after they had gathered, Pilate said to them, "Whom do you want me to release for you, Jesus Barabbas or Jesus who is called the Messiah?"* ¹⁸ *For he realized that it was out of jealousy that they had handed him over.*

Pilate was an attentive politician who had aspirations of furthering his career. As part of supervising the Passover celebration, he would have typically used the prisoner release to create goodwill with the people. Usually the prisoner was someone whose crime had not been too serious and who was popular with the public. He apparently thought that with Jesus' popularity among the people, the crowd would demand his release, thus saving Pilate from a difficult situation. But little did he know the determination of the religious leaders who were directing the electrified crowd, orchestrating the outcome he sought to avoid

Read Matthew 27:19.

While he [Pilate] was sitting on the judgment seat, his wife sent word to him, "Have nothing to do with that innocent man, for today I have suffered a great deal because of a dream about him."

It would not have been surprising for Pilate's wife to have had a disturbing dream about Jesus in the days after his arrival in the city via the Palm Branch Parade. But it would have been exceedingly rare for her to have acted on such a dream. It is dumbfounding that she attempted to influence the head of her household about a major political decision—especially one that involved such huge crowds and had a significant potential for riots.

It's possible, likely even, that Pilate's wife had heard about Jesus. She may have seen part of the impromptu parade from the high vantage point of her home in the city. She may also have heard Jesus teach in the streets of Jerusalem or been aware of the miracles he was performing. "Legend tells us that…she showed interest in the Judaistic faith of the people whom her husband ruled" (ibid., page 596). We don't know specifically why she took the risk, but this unnamed woman spoke out of turn to a man in significant power because she was so moved by her dreams of the Messiah.

Read Matthew 27:20-23.

Now the chief priests and the elders persuaded the crowds to ask for Barabbas and to have Jesus killed. ²¹ *The governor again said to them,*

"Which of the two do you want me to release for you?" And they said, "Barabbas." [22] Pilate said to them, "Then what should I do with Jesus who is called the Messiah?" All of them said, "Let him be crucified!" [23] Then he asked, "Why, what evil has he done?" But they shouted all the more, "Let him be crucified!"

While it sounds as if everyone in the crowd was shouting against Jesus, the religious leaders had planted people throughout the crowd to serve as antagonists. Jesus' true friends and followers would not have had a chance against this crowd.

There was little evidence to support the accusations against Jesus, but Pilate "was sparring for time, vacillating as to his own course. In his fear of [Emperor] Tiberius he could neither condone treason nor punish the innocent. In his hatred for the temple leaders he had no wish to do their desire, but he had still to consult his own interests. He hoped that the crowd might plead for the release of Jesus" (ibid., page 597).

Read Matthew 27:24-26.

So when Pilate saw that he could do nothing, but rather that a riot was beginning, he took some water and washed his hands before the crowd, saying, "I am innocent of this man's blood; see to it yourselves." [25] *Then the people as a whole answered, "His blood be on us and on our children!"* [26] *So he released Barabbas for them; and after flogging Jesus, he handed him over to be crucified.*

Pilate had a strong desire to protect his political standing and the station that he had achieved in his military and political career. Keeping the people he governed under control and enabling his messengers to send peaceful reports to his superiors in regional capital cities seemed to be his priority.

In the end, despite the warnings from his wife, Pilate issued the execution order for the innocent man Jesus and the release order for a notorious criminal Jesus. While he attempted publicly to avoid any responsibility for the surprising turn of events by washing his hands, the responsibility for Jesus' crucifixion and Jesus Barabbas' release both rest squarely with him.

Scenic Route

As governor of Judea, Pilate was a part of the Roman government hierarchy. Ultimately, his primary role was to keep peace and command a medium-sized battalion of Roman soldiers. He would have enforced the laws, collected the taxes, and squashed any revolts. Anything he couldn't handle, Pilate would have referred to the legions located nearby in Syria and/or the Prefect, who commanded them.

When have you tried to stand up for what you believed to be right despite being in the minority? How was your opinion received?

In what situations have you seen people protecting their own interests at the expense of others' welfare?

Where do you see the avoidance of responsibility in today's world? How does this practice affect others?

Given that Pilate's wife was willing to speak out about Jesus, what would you say about the strength of her convictions?

How do family members often influence decisions today, even those decisions that affect people outside the family?

What difference does how one approaches a situation often make? How can you most effectively influence others?

However, an admission of failure to control the people was to be avoided at all costs.

When a Roman governor relocated a significant distance, he was allowed to take his wife and any children, provided it was safe for him to do so. Matthew's account is the only one to mention Pilate's wife. This woman is given no name in the biblical account and, in fact, only exists for this one verse, but she had a unique voice in this drama. To understand the seriousness of her actions, we need to know more about a woman's life during ancient times.

A woman had no rights within the household structure in Roman and Greek times. The male head of household was called the paterfamilias (*pater*—father, *familias*—family). The men in those roles were the only Roman citizens who could own property, hold office, or have any power. While women were allowed to be Roman citizens, they were to defer entirely to their *paterfamilias*, whether that be their father, husband, or possibly other male relative. The *paterfamilias* even had the power of life and death over all members of the household, including their wives and children.

These cultural norms did change slightly as a man (and his family) rose to prominence within the hierarchy of the Roman world. The women of the upper class (of which Pilate's wife was most certainly a member) were subtly able to influence their husbands, fathers, and other men through their work and service. In these families, husbands often gave their wives oversight of the servants and slaves and the lands where they lived. However, it was exceedingly rare for a woman to have any notable political power (be able to speak to or direct the actions of governors, the senate, or anyone else in leadership) or, more specifically, to advise their husbands or fathers in their administrative or leadership roles.

It is worth noting how Pilate's wife intruded into the decision-making process. While her interruption was entirely out of line with how such decisions were typically made, she didn't show up in the court (where there were certainly zero women present) to make her case. Instead, she sensitively relayed the message to her husband via a messenger, most probably a male servant of her household, whose presence with Pilate would have been normal and even expected.

Workers Ahead

There continues to be a significant number of people throughout the world who don't have a voice in decisions that affect them. Most often these people are women. Even in the United States, many women do not have an equal voice. These women struggle to get equal pay for the same work as their male counterparts. They are often single parent heads of household and may not have had access to the same quality of education. In developing countries, the situation is more dire.

Organizations such as Fair Trade, Thistle Farm Global, Women's Empowerment International, the United Nations, and others are working to help women have a voice. True empowerment comes in being able to control one's own destiny. With access to markets for their products, fair prices being paid for merchandise, increased availability to education and healthcare, women have more of voice in the world. Some of these organizations also provide loans to help women start small businesses.

By working for the betterment of all people, we are sharing our faith in Jesus. Just as Pilate's wife took an unpopular stance by encouraging her husband to release Jesus, supporting efforts and organizations such as those listed above may not be popular with segments of our population, possibly not within our communities or even our families. However, followers of Jesus are not known for waiting patiently for an invitation to speak or act. At the same time, we must be careful not to offend people, which could result in more harm than good.

Of what groups are you aware that work to better conditions for women and others who are vulnerable? How do these groups give people a voice?

In the Rear View

One of Pilate's closest family members intruded into his decision making, even when she wasn't wanted. When we are faced with the decision of whether or not to share our faith with someone, consider your relationship with that person. The closer your relationship, the more likely it is your words will be heard and considered.

Learning to speak in the moment of someone's spiritual need is a skill that is sometimes difficult to develop. Knowing what to say and how to say it further complicates the matter and often the relationship. As you close your time together, share the prayer below. Ask God to guide you as to when and where to speak up about your faith, even if your gender, your authority, or your power might suggest you be quiet.

Almighty and gracious God, We think about acting, about using our voices for you. Move within us through your spirit, O God, and give us your voice and your words so that we speak truth in love. Give us the boldness of Pilate's wife so that our words might be spoken, even to those in our own families. Amen.

In what instances do you need to speak out of turn?

Travel Log

Day 1:

    Recall a time when you wanted to speak up about something but felt it wasn't your place to do so. How might the situation have turned out differently if you had not remained silent? Journal your thoughts about that time.

Day 2:

    Think about people you know, as well as people throughout the world, who are subjected to the dominance of others. What is your responsibility in such situations? To whom might God be calling you to speak? Identify people who have the power to address some of these situations (government leaders, community organizations, etc.) and write a letter to them that explains your concerns. Continue to seek action until changes are made.

Day 3:

For the last several years, the United States has witnessed an increasing number of protests, some of which have become riotous mobs. Consider your feelings about the reasons for these protests. Make some notes about how you can make a difference so that people no longer feel the need for such protests. For instance, you might want to write editorials to local newspapers, create a blog, etc.

Day 4:

In what instances has your gender prevented you from having a voice in a conversation or a decision? Why do you think Matthew included this particular moment in his Gospel? Jot down a few ideas as to how you can offer all people a voice.

Day 5:

Investigate the women's empowerment organizations listed in the lesson or find out about some in your own community. Learn how you can become involved in their efforts. Plan how you can share their mission with others.

Day 6:

Who in your sphere of influence might benefit greatly from your faith? What has kept you from sharing your faith with them? List the names of these people and some possible ways of sharing your faith with them.

Day 7:

God revealed Jesus' innocence to Pilate's wife, who spoke boldly on Jesus' behalf. For whom is God calling you to speak boldly? To whom is God calling you to speak? Make some notes about how you will respond to God's call.

From a Distance

Scripture for lesson: Mark 15:40-41

Written by Steven Shelton

When have you been told that you should or could not do something because of your gender? In academics, sports, technology, hobbies, and even in churches and religious settings, our culture creates expectations for males and females. How have you violated those norms and expectations?

It's no surprise that males and females are different. According to psychological research, intellectually and socially our capacities for intelligence, creativity, relationships, and leadership are nearly identical. Yet at the same time, the approaches that men and women typically utilize to learn, grow, work, and connect are often quite different.

A great example is an average road trip for our family. Usually I am the default driver for all family trips. However, when the drive time exceeds three or four hours, my wife shares the responsibility and drudgery of driving. Whoever is behind the wheel is responsible for operating the vehicle; the one in the passenger seat is responsible for musical entertainment, snacks, our girls, and most importantly: navigation. During long trips while transitioning between driving and navigating, our approaches to driving become more apparent.

If I am driving, I need to know how far it is until my next turn. My wife would rather know the name of the road onto which she needs to turn.

If I am driving, I tend to know the location of our vehicle in relation to all the other vehicles within a few hundred yards. She tends to know the location of our vehicle in relation to the notable landmarks around us and where we are in a city.

If I am driving, I would rather see a map with my direction and speed. She would rather see a list of directions that details the turns and the order in which they occur.

If we are traveling a somewhat familiar route, I can look at the map and know the route. She navigates without ever seeing a map, using only landmarks.

Generally speaking, I'm better with spatial awareness while she is better with factual understanding, but it's important to note that while our approaches are different, we've both learned that the other is just as effective. It's taken many, many years of marriage to learn how to communicate precisely what the other person needs to know while behind the wheel, but we always manage to get there, regardless of who is driving, even when we lose our GPS signal or cell connection.

However, the very real differences that exist between men and women are partly natural occurrences that come out of our created uniqueness, but others are culturally created and socially enforced. When I was in elementary school, I remember one of the girls bringing Teen Talk Barbie to class. This doll would make headlines that year because one of its potential phrases, "Math class is tough" reinforced the idea that girls were not as good at math as the boys were. The stories that each generation tells its children become that next generation's reality. If we're told that we can't, we won't, and if we're told that we can, we will.

Prep for the Journey

Punishment for crimes in ancient times was quite different from what we in more developed nations know and experience today. While jails were used in Jesus' time, as evidenced by both Peter and Paul being imprisoned, most often they were places where criminals were held only until sentencing was pronounced. Individuals who had access to funds were sometimes banished to an island or very remote city for an indefinite period of time, usually for life. If they ever returned home, they were subject to death. John, who wrote the Book of Revelation, received this sentence.

Minor crimes, especially the white collar variety, were punishable by fine, the confiscation of property, or possible enslavement for the repayment of a debt. Land confiscation was a favorite target of many a greedy and corrupt governor of the time. Those who were poor or who had nothing to confiscate were often subjected to beatings, lashings, and other non-lethal physical punishments.

Individuals found guilty of serious theft or crimes of passion were sentenced to a death-causing variety of punishment: sent to the gladiatorial arena, sold as slaves, conscripted to work in government-run mines, or placed as oarsmen in Roman warships. Alternatively, when death itself was the desired outcome, Roman authorities beheaded, burned alive, and strangled prisoners. Sometimes they allowed a captured, low ranking soldier a noble suicide.

But for the worst of the worst criminals (enemies of the state, captured rebels and instigators of war, etc.) combinations of beatings and executions were used. In those situations, the most painful and degrading type of death would be extracted from the criminal: crucifixion. A crucifixion was both excruciatingly slow and painful, but also public and humiliating (nailed naked to a pole in a very public place). "Execution by crucifixion began immediately after conviction and sentencing was pronounced. Flogging usually preceded the

How have you been affected by the idea that boys were better at some things and girls better at others?

How do you feel about punishment for crimes in the United States? What changes would you suggest?

procession to the outskirts of the city. A route was chosen that would attract as much attention as possible, for the crowd would often follow to witness the execution" (*The Land and People Jesus Knew*, by J. Robert Teringo, © 1985, page 239).

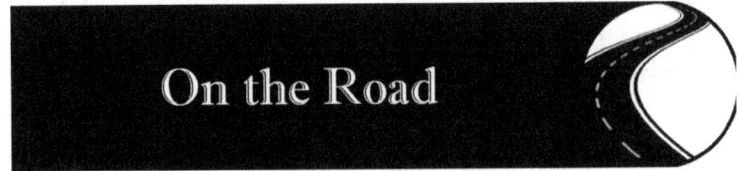

On the Road

The previous lesson ended with Pilate sentencing Jesus to die by crucifixion. Jesus' followers had scattered, fearing for their own lives because of their association with Jesus. However, some of his followers watched from a distance. These followers were the ones most unlikely to have been present.

Read Mark 15:40-41.
There were also women looking on from a distance; among them were Mary Magdalene, and Mary the mother of James the younger and of Joses, and Salome. [41] These used to follow him and provided for him when he was in Galilee; and there were many other women who had come up with him to Jerusalem.

These women were powerless to do anything to stop the crucifixion of their beloved teacher, but there were things they could and did do. "For one thing they saw that this was a monstrous wrong and did not condone it.…In the second place the defeat on Calvary did not shake their faith in Jesus or their devotion to him.…They continued as an unshaken minority, a minority that became God's instrument for the future" (*The Interpreter's Bible, Vol. 7*, © 1951, page 908). To have condoned Jesus' crucifixion would have been like saying that perhaps the authorities were right, that he deserved to die. Such feelings occur when people mistake might for right. These women continued to be loyal to Jesus despite the power of those who opposed him. What a wonderful testimony to their belief in and love for Jesus!

These particular women had traveled with Jesus during his ministry. Because Passover was celebrated in family units, with both men and women present, it would not have been uncommon for women to have made the journey to Jerusalem. The Passover meal would likely have been prepared by these (and perhaps many other) women who were among Jesus' followers.

Women were allowed to conduct business and to make occasional excursions to the marketplace, but were largely relegated to a life at home, rarely allowed to leave. It is very surprising that these women were present at an execution, especially without the presence of their "men folk." As you imagine the women of this passage present at Jesus' crucifixion, remember the gruesomeness of the scene they were

When have you seen extreme courage from an unlikely source?

How do you feel knowing that these women stayed close to Jesus when the disciples fled?

In what situations do you currently see people condoning wrong rather than standing against them?

Imagine yourself as one of the women watching the crucifixion. What thoughts are going through your mind?

witnessing. However, the fact that they were "at a distance" may have had more to do with their presence at a men-only event than with the gruesome nature of what they were viewing.

Although Mark does not say anything about these women being part of a group of followers who had gathered to witness the crucifixion, other men were in attendance—Jewish leaders, townspeople, Passover visitors, etc.—who should have noticed that the women were present when and where they should not have been. It is curious that none of these men challenged the women's presence. That these women were left alone to be present for something they should not have attended is a testament to their determination and their resolve to be loyal to Jesus.

Scenic Route

Jesus welcomed women and children, which was practically unheard of at the time; other teachers discounted both groups. Throughout the Gospels, Jesus often addressed or supported the roles of women—allowing them to worship him as he ate (Mary Magdalene and the precious perfume), allowing them to be present as he taught, and even inviting them into roles of discipleship.

All of the Gospels mention that women were present for Jesus' crucifixion, but John is the only one that specifically mentions the presence of any of the disciples: "Jesus saw his mother and the disciple whom he loved standing beside her" (19:26). Luke says that Jesus' "acquaintances, including the women who had followed him from Galilee, stood at a distance" (23:49). The fact that women were mentioned by all four Gospel writers indicates the significance of their presence.

At the close of Mark 15, we see that these same women remained present until Jesus' body was placed in the tomb and the tomb was sealed. It is likely that they had followed Jesus' every step that day. Just imagine the danger in which these dedicated followers placed themselves. Unescorted women were at risk of being accused of promiscuity or of being victimized, yet they stayed until the end.

Modern scholarship is finding that women likely had a much larger role in the spread of the early church than first thought. They were teachers and missionaries; they opened their homes as meeting places for followers of Jesus; and they supported Jesus' ministry financially. Many women were drawn to the gospel message because of it gave hope for those who were "the least of these," and women certainly fell into the category. Often the women expressed their faith and devotion through social service ministries. They gave generously of their funds and selflessly of their time and energy.

What are you willing to disregard or sacrifice in order to be present for Christ?

When have you not been present for a friend in need? How did you feel afterward?

Why do you think Jesus' male followers, who had the right and authority to be present at the trial and the crucifixion, were not visible during Jesus' final hours? What do you think prompted the women to be present despite the moral and social sanctions they would likely endure?

The lives of women today, especially in the United States, are quite different from the ancient women who are the subject of our lesson. In what ways are the lives of women different, but more interestingly, in what ways are their lives still relatively the same?

Workers Ahead

The Cumberland Presbyterian Church has recognized the role of women in leadership from a very early time (several decades before women in the United States were able to vote). Despite the pride we have in being the first of the Reformed family of denominations to ordain women as preachers, starting with Louisa Woosley in 1889, today men are far more often selected as the pastors of Cumberland Presbyterian congregations than are women.

While Louisa's journey was not easy, she followed God's call. Thankfully, the Cumberland Presbyterian denomination was able to see God at work in her life. After being licensed to preach by Nolin Presbytery in Kentucky Synod, Louisa preached 267 sermons and witnessed 306 professions of faith with 119 additions to the church. When presbytery received her ministerial record for the previous year, they appointed her as presbyterial missionary, giving her the freedom to evangelize anywhere within the bounds of the presbytery during the following year.

Two years after presenting herself as a candidate, she was ordained by Nolin Presbytery. When the synod reviewed its presbyteries' minutes, they claimed that neither the Bible nor the *Confession of Faith* gave them authority for such actions. The motion to revoke Louisa's ordination died for lack of a second.

Talented and capable women abound in our congregations. They are dedicated to the work of our churches—serving, teaching, and leading in every area of ministry. Many churches encourage young women to explore God's call for their lives, which may be volunteer or professional. These women have gifts and they should not have to be at a distance from where any of God's work is occurring.

> What keeps our churches' actions from matching our history and our doctrine? How readily would your church accept the leadership of a female pastor?

> What keeps women from being able to use their gifts in your congregation? How can that situation be addressed?

In the Rear View

Women have been an important part of the Christian church from its beginnings. They have fought societal norms in order to do the work to which God has called them. They have shown great courage by remaining faithful in the face of extreme peril. We give thanks for their examples and sacrifices!

Gracious God, give us the courage of these women so that we will speak even when others may not think we should have a voice. Show us those who need to hear your voice through us so. Help us to offer encouragement to those who are struggling to find their voice. Amen.

Travel Log

Day 1:

What differences, other than physical, do you notice between human males and females? How do these differences cause you to treat someone differently? As you reflect on these questions, draw or jot down some ideas.

Day 2:

Jesus told us that when we minister to those who are in prison, we are ministering to him. Often we are hesitant to become involved with people who are incarcerated. How might you and/or your group be able to share God's love with people who are in jail? Make some notes and share your ideas with others.

Day 3:

Think about a time when you were somewhere that you probably should not have been. Maybe you walked into a meeting to which you had not been invited. Perhaps you did not enter the correct room at the funeral parlor when going to pay your respects to a friend. You may have even interjected yourself into a group that had denied you access. Compare your feelings at that time to how the women may have felt as, from a distance, they watched the proceedings of Jesus' final day.

Day 4:

How does the story of Louisa Woosley make you feel about being part of the Cumberland Presbyterian Church? Journal your thoughts. Then spend time in prayer, thanking God for women who were and are not afraid to follow God's call.

Day 5:

Identify the women in your church who accept leadership roles. Write them a note of appreciation and encouragement.

Day 6:

Unfortunately, some talented and dedicated women are not given the opportunity to use their gifts and talents benefit of God's kingdom. Consider the women in your faith circle. What are their gifts? How does the church encourage them to use those gifts? Write down some words of encouragement that you will share with these women.

Day 7:

List the women in your life whose examples have impacted your faith development. Write a prayer of thanks for these women. If they are still living, write them a note of thanks.

A Not-So-Secret Disciple

Scripture for lesson: Matthew 27:57-60

Written by Steven Shelton

There are times when most of us hesitate to share openly our true thoughts or feelings. During the most recent election, many people remained silent rather than be subjected to a barrage of comments from someone whom they knew held opposing views.

While silence may help us to survive a difficult situation, it is not always the best strategy. When we fail to speak up about something that is important or about which we have strong feelings, we are not being true to ourselves. We may also be allowing injustices to occur because we are hesitant to speak against those who are in control or who are more powerful.

Prep for the Journey

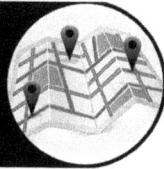

Joseph of Arimathea is mentioned in all of the Gospels, mostly because he provided the tomb in which Jesus was buried, which indicated that he was a man of some means. The parallel passage in Mark 15:48 refers to Joseph as honorable. Mark also described Joseph as a member of the council, which could have been a local group or the Sanhedrin. Luke's account tells us that Joseph had not agreed to the council's plan and action, giving credence to the idea that he was a member of the Sanhedrin. According to Mark, Joseph was a pious Jew, "who hoped for the kingdom of God and therefore might be sympathetic to Jesus' teaching" (*The Interpreter's Bible, Vol. 7,* © 1951, page 612).

It is likely that Joseph voiced his concern over Jesus' trial and was out voted by his fellow council members. But disagreements among leaders was not uncommon. However, Joseph went beyond voicing any concerns to take care of Jesus' body so that Jewish law was not violated. Through his very visible actions, Joseph showed that he was not ashamed of his loyalty to the Messiah.

When has your position (job, leadership role, relationship to your church) caused you not to act or speak when you should have?

How can being pious sometimes get in the way of following God?

When have you voiced serious concerns only to be out voted. How did you react? In what ways were you able to continue to voice concerns?

When have you been called upon to do a necessary task when no one else was available?

What laws/customs apply to funerals/burials in your community?

What assumptions might people make based on your associations with other people?

What personal possessions have you been willing to sacrifice so that others can have what they need?

On the Road

It was late in the day and Jesus was dead. Despite the desertion of Jesus' followers and disciples, there was a pressing question on the minds of all those who did not run away: "What will we do with Jesus' body?" Jesus' relatives were from Galilee. None of them owned any land near Jerusalem, much less had access to a tomb in the area. Taking care of his body after the execution was a need that many of the disciples likely overlooked in their haste to escape the trial and anticipated persecution.

Read Matthew 27:57-60.

When it was evening, there came a rich man from Arimathea, named Joseph, who was also a disciple of Jesus. [58] He went to Pilate and asked for the body of Jesus; then Pilate ordered it to be given to him. [59] So Joseph took the body and wrapped it in a clean linen cloth [60] and laid it in his own new tomb, which he had hewn in the rock. He then rolled a great stone to the door of the tomb and went away.

There were two laws that affected Jesus' remains. Roman law said that the body of an executed criminal could be released only to relatives. If no relatives claimed the body, it was left to hang on the cross until animals took care of the remains. Since Rome was the ruling power, that law came first; any subsequent local or religious laws could only be followed if they did not violate the Roman law.

The second law, and the one more important for Jesus' situation, was the Jewish law. Deuteronomy 21:22-23 states that a body could not be left to hang after an execution. The deceased must be buried before the sun set. Jesus died in the late afternoon, so there was not much time for his family or followers to tend to his burial.

According to the Sanhedrin, the ruling Jewish council, Jesus was a criminal. Anyone claiming his body who wasn't a relative would most certainly have been a disciple. This person would have stood a great chance of being arrested and then punished, just for being associated with Jesus.

The solution to the complicated problem of Jesus' burial came in the form of a man named Joseph, who may have been a follower of Jesus. Joseph was originally from Arimathea, but his ownership of a tomb in Jerusalem tells us that he had relocated to that city. He likely had purchased the tomb in anticipation of his own needs.

Joseph had a lot to lose by stepping up to take responsibility for Jesus' body, but that didn't stop him. Joseph went to see Pilate and requested permission to take Jesus' body. There is a slight possibility that Joseph was a distant relative, which would have given him authority to claim the body, or he may have used his wealth to circumvent the relationship requirement. In full view of everyone, he ascended the hill of Golgotha and took possession of Jesus' remains. He took those remains, carefully wrapped them in a clean linen shroud according to the Jewish customs and specifications, and placed Jesus' body in a tomb he had bought for his own use.

Scenic Route

"Burial took place in tombs and sepulchers, or in natural caves. For those who couldn't afford even a cave site, a simple grave would be used. Tombs and sepulchers were hand-hewn out of the soft limestone hillsides that abound in Palestine. Most tombs had more than one chamber, with the forecourt serving as a vestibule for relatives to mourn....the other room(s) were burial chambers with small platforms, like extended fingers carved into the walls for laying the bodies. The door to such a burial chamber was a removable stone slab. A large round stone disc that would be rolled into place was used to seal the tomb entrance" (*The Land and People Jesus Knew*, by J. Robert Teringo, © 1985, page 217).

In ancient times, tombs were family affairs. In wealthy families, as was apparently true for Joseph, tombs were large and were expected to be used for the burial of many generations. Poorer families had smaller tombs, making do with what space they had. In these smaller tombs, it was common for bodies to be laid quite close to one another and for the remains to be moved slightly to make room for the newly dead. But of particular note, rich or poor, once a family began using a tomb, it was not to be sold or used by anyone not a member of the family.

For Joseph to bury Jesus in his own tomb was a great sacrifice. If, as we think, Joseph was not related to Jesus, none of Joseph's family could have been buried there. It was also forbidden to bury one's family members in the same tomb as an executed man. Regardless of the relationship, Joseph's decision to offer his tomb as the burial place of Jesus would have had far reaching consequences in his business, social standing, and role in the Sanhedrin. In whatever way he was or was not related to Jesus, incredible risk was associated with his actions.

What important task have you done that others were too hesitant, afraid, or embarrassed to do? Why were you willing to do it, especially if it could have personal ramifications?

Traditional burials have become very expensive. How are the burials of poorer people handled in your community?

What risks do you face because of those with whom you associate or because of the stances you take?

When has the expression "Things can always be worse" come true for you? How often do you take for granted how good things are? In light of seeing yourself compared to the rest of the world, how rich do you feel?

What about these statistics surprises you? What is your personal responsibility to the world's poor? How can/should the church respond?

What role do you think money plays in preventing obvious and visible discipleship or activity in your city? in your country?

While in college, I had a job that gave me just enough extra cash to do the things I needed to be able to do. However, it was common for me to have to skip pizza night with the guys, rent a movie rather than go to the theater, and ride my bike the two miles to class because I didn't want to spend the gas money. Through it all, there were moments when, though I recognized my blessings at receiving an education and never being hungry, I felt quite poor.

My Job was in childcare with elementary-aged students every morning and two afternoons a week, which gave me about 15 hours a week. I also earned minimum wage, which was only $5.15 an hour in Tennessee. If you do some quick math, my income was roughly $65-70 a week after taxes. If you divide that across a full week, it comes to about $10 per day. Considering that I didn't have to pay rent or tuition and ate 15 meals a week in the cafeteria, $10 a day wasn't terrible. (The adjusted amount for 2017 is $13 a day.) I'm sorry to bore you with all those numbers, but I wanted us to have a familiar point of reference before we jump into our next point.

Pew Research has put together a snapshot of world poverty, and the results are startling. They describe the people of the world as divided among 5 different groups: the poor and the low income, middle income, upper-middle income, and high income. The poor are defined as living on $2 or less a day, low-income as living on $2-$10 a day, middle income as living on $10-20 a day, upper-middle as living on $20-50 a day, and high income individuals as anything above $50 per day. While in the United States, these figures would have put me (during college) in the bottom 10-12 percent of people, globally speaking, I would easily have been within the top 30 percent.

Billions and billions of people, the vast majority (70 percent) of humanity, lives on less than what that part-time college student earned working for minimum wage. In other words, you are part of the high income bracket of the Pew Research if you earn at least $8.77 per hour in a 40 hour a week job.

In the United States, we take for granted that even those who are considered to be poor are statistically better off than more than half the world. In so many places, hundreds of millions of people are anxiously looking not just for their next meal, but for where they can be safe from war, corruption, and disease.

It is nearly always difficult to put our faith before our finances. Living in this wealthy and prosperous country means that the stock market report is a regular part of nearly every newscast. We are surrounded each day by advertisements of all the different things one can buy. The people who are using those advertised items seem so happy!

Our possessions, our income, our wealth all have the potential to come between us and God. Jesus warns us about this repeatedly through the Gospels and speaks on money more often than almost any other topic. We should be very aware of how dangerous our money can become. Will you seek a promotion rather than an opportunity to follow God's purpose for your life? Will you use what you do have to gain more possessions and prestige rather than contribute to the work of God's kingdom?

Long ago God set the tithe (ten percent) as the standard for what we are to give back to God. Scholars and pastors (and church treasurers!) debate as to whether the tithe is based on gross or net income and about whether it applies only to your local church or to denominational giving, but any way you look at it, research shows that Christians in the United States on average give 2.43 percent, less than a quarter of a tithe. It would be a sad luxury for us to be able to participate in the net versus gross debate when most of us aren't even close.

In the Rear View

The generosity of a rich man may tempt us to lessen the significance of his gift by noting only his wealth, lamenting how easy it would be to give if only we had more. God doesn't ask us to acquire and then to serve and be faithful. God does not have an income line above which we give and below which we continue only to serve ourselves.

Almighty and gracious God, give us the generosity of Joseph so that we might be able to speak through our finances, through our sacrifice, and through our commitment to your kingdom, sharing our resources with those who have none. Amen.

Why is it so hard for believers in the richest country in the history of all humanity to give what we are asked to give? How much does the extravagant gift of Joseph surprise you? inspire you? What things could you sacrifice so that you can give more to the work God does through your congregation?

How might we match Joseph's generosity?

Travel Log

Day 1:

Do your own research. Google more about the differences between the rich and the poor. Write down any statements that floor you and post them where you will see them every day. When you see the statements, say a brief prayer of thanks for your blessings.

Day 2:

When have you been concerned about what the right thing was to do in a situation? Write a few words to describe what you did. Record your true feelings then and now.

Day 3:

Write a poem about Joseph of Arimathea and his commitment to Jesus. Your poem doesn't have to rhyme or be fancy; just raise up the qualities that made him someone to emulate.

Day 4:

When have you had to sacrifice your standing, or that of your family, in your community? Journal about your feelings, frustrations, fears, etc.

Day 5:

List the ways you put your faith before your finances.

Day 6:

Google the program "40 Bags in 40 Days." If you are interested in trying this program, make a list of the areas in your home and life that you want to target. Say a brief prayer that this process will be spiritual as well as physical.

Day 7:

Tabulate your current percentage of giving to the church. Start there and figure what it would look like to increase your giving by a percentage. Continue to tabulate until you reach 10 percent. If you are already at 10 percent, consider giving beyond that point. Plan to pray daily about increasing your giving to discern if God is calling you to do so.

A Luxurious Gift

Scripture for lesson: John 3:1-17; 19:39-40

Written by Steven Shelton

When did you decide to do something only to end up "in over your head"? When have you ended up in such a situation as a result of something you felt God was calling you to do? How did you handle it? How difficult was it to continue when things became complicated?

Early last year, I was so very excited to be able to purchase my first-ever new car. It was of the small SUV variety. I was excited to have more cargo/leg/head/car seat room than I had had in the compact car that I had been driving for about 10 years. During the first several months of owning my new ride, I took extra special care of it, keeping it cleaned out, washing it regularly, and absolutely not allowing anyone's food to come anywhere near it.

Somewhere in the third month of owning my new vehicle, I had a small project to do at home that required me to purchase some wood. I was ecstatic to be able to fold down the seats and use all that brand new cargo room. So, I drove my new SUV to the local hardware store. I had heard that this particular store would pre-cut wood, but when I asked for the employee who would do so, I got only blank stares and redirections to other employees. After wandering around the store and talking to six different people, I finally found the guy I needed, but he said they no longer provided this service. After several minutes of persistence and persuasion, he reluctantly agreed to cut my wood.

After making the purchase, I pushed the unwieldy cart out to my car and immediately noticed that getting all of the wood into it would not be easy. The longest pieces would have to sit on the driver's seat armrest, extending almost all the way to the front windshield. Each piece would need to be placed carefully so that all the other pieces would fit. I started laying them in one after another, removing some and re-situating others. After pushing and pulling and shoving, my SUV was beginning to get quite full and I began to see some weird colorations on the front ceiling of my still new-smelling vehicle. Taking a break, I left the last few pieces of wood in the cart and went to investigate the colored marks, which is how I discovered that saw mills apply a chalk-like substance to different cuts of wood to tell them apart easily.

I sat in a dazed stupor, staring at the bright blue lines across the interior roof of my Brand. New. Car. I was so mad. I could not believe the difficulties I had faced. I was well more than an hour into this ordeal and now my car ceiling was stained. I very, very carefully loaded the last few pieces into my vehicle and managed to put only one more blue spot on my ceiling through the unloading process at home.

Often, we approach a task, a project, or an event with an expectation of what it will cost us and how difficult it may be, and we hope and pray that those expectations are met. But sometimes it just doesn't work out.

Prep for the Journey

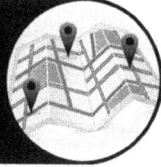

Nicodemus is a name that appears early in Jesus' ministry, once briefly in the middle of Jesus' ministry, and again after Jesus' death. Even though Nicodemus was a Pharisee, he became a "seeker"—one who saw something in Jesus and wanted to know more.

Read John 3:1-17.

Now there was a Pharisee named Nicodemus, a leader of the Jews. ² He came to Jesus by night and said to him, "Rabbi, we know that you are a teacher who has come from God; for no one can do these signs that you do apart from the presence of God." ³ Jesus answered him, "Very truly, I tell you, no one can see the kingdom of God without being born from above." ⁴ Nicodemus said to him, "How can anyone be born after having grown old? Can one enter a second time into the mother's womb and be born?" ⁵ Jesus answered, "Very truly, I tell you, no one can enter the kingdom of God without being born of water and Spirit. ⁶ What is born of the flesh is flesh, and what is born of the Spirit is spirit. ⁷ Do not be astonished that I said to you, 'You must be born from above.' ⁸ The wind blows where it chooses, and you hear the sound of it, but you do not know where it comes from or where it goes. So it is with everyone who is born of the Spirit." ⁹ Nicodemus said to him, "How can these things be?" ¹⁰ Jesus answered him, "Are you a teacher of Israel, and yet you do not understand these things?

¹¹ "Very truly, I tell you, we speak of what we know and testify to what we have seen; yet you do not receive our testimony. ¹² If I have told you about earthly things and you do not believe, how can you believe if I tell you about heavenly things? ¹³ No one has ascended into heaven except the one who descended from heaven, the Son of Man. ¹⁴ And just as Moses lifted up the serpent in the wilderness, so must the Son of Man be lifted up, ¹⁵ that whoever believes in him may have eternal life.

¹⁶ "For God so loved the world that he gave his only Son, so that everyone who believes in him may not perish but may have eternal life.

¹⁷ "Indeed, God did not send the Son into the world to condemn the world, but in order that the world might be saved through him.

Nicodemus was the man to whom Jesus spoke the best known and most often quoted verse in all of scripture, John 3:16. It was said at night, likely in a private conversation between Nicodemus and

> When have your expectations not matched reality? How did you react to the difference between hope and reality?
>
> How does your church reach out to those who are "seekers" in today's world?
>
> How does it feel to know that some of Jesus' best known words were spoken in a secret meeting in the dark of night?

When have you failed to understand something that should have been obvious to one in your position? What ultimately brought clarity?

When have you known you needed to make a decision on something, yet you waited a very long time to confirm or openly confess that decision? What made you wait? What made you finally decide to admit and/or share what you had decided?

Jesus. Jesus challenged Nicodemus' role as a Pharisee and an elder of the Jewish people by asking, "Are you a teacher of Israel, and yet you do not understand?"

Their conversation ended shortly thereafter, and Jesus left Jerusalem (where he was visiting to celebrate the Passover) to continue his ministry in Galilee. It is possible that, like Joseph of Arimathea, Nicodemus was a member of the Sanhedrin. Whatever his role, he was known well enough that he felt it was necessary to visit Jesus at night, hiding his visit from the populace and his fellow Pharisees. Nicodemus likely lived in or near Jerusalem.

On the Road

Read John 19:39-40.

Nicodemus, who had at first come to Jesus by night, also came, bringing a mixture of myrrh and aloes, weighing about a hundred pounds. [40] They took the body of Jesus and wrapped it with the spices in linen cloths, according to the burial custom of the Jews.

Something happened within Nicodemus to move him from a questioning night visitor to the Messiah to a bold caretaker of Jesus' body. Like Joseph of Arimathea, Nicodemus was known among the Jewish leadership in Jerusalem; however, unlike Joseph, Nicodemus' life as a Pharisee would have put him in a difficult place both from a theological perspective (did he believe Jesus really was the Messiah) and as a spiritual leader (how would the other Pharisees respond to his actions).

Nicodemus would have been faced with the prospect of continuing to hide his growing belief in Jesus the Messiah of Jewish prophecy (despite the vehement thoughts to the contrary of many of his Pharisee companions), or stepping out to finish the journey he began on that dark night many years ago. There are moments within any spiritual journey that will determine the course of the future journey. Despite the struggles of his journey, he chose to follow Christ publicly, even when so many disciples chose to abandon him.

Scenic Route

We know from the last lesson that Joseph of Arimathea provided something necessary and practical for Jesus in his hour of need: a tomb. This gift was very costly in terms of money and social/religious standing. Even though the Jewish authorities understood that someone needed to provide for Jesus' burial, anyone who did so was suspect, especially one from their own ranks. Eventually someone in authority would have arranged for Jesus to be buried nearby and inexpensively. Even though Joseph went above and beyond what was necessary, his actions could still have been considered as simply making sure the law was followed.

Nicodemus, however, provided something that moved beyond necessity into the realm of luxury. Any person buried in ancient times was anointed with sweet smelling spices and oils, which were to mask the eventual odors that would accompany decomposition. When a person died, "the eyes were closed, the entire body was washed and anointed with oil, and the hands and feet were then wrapped in linen bands. The body…was then wrapped around with winding sheets. Spices of myrrh and aloes were placed in the folds of the garment to perfume the body" (*The Land and People Jesus Knew*, by J. Robert Teringo © 1985, page 217).

This anointing was typically done shortly after death. The cloths absorbed the oils and retained the fragrance of the spices, somewhat sealing in the decay of the body. In a normal burial, only a cup or two of scented oils was used, which was probably all that a common laborer could have afforded. In cases of an important, wealthy, or royal figure being buried, as much as several gallons of oils were used to ensure a long lasting scent and complete covering of the body for many weeks or months.

John tells his readers that Nicodemus brought 100 pounds of myrrh and aloes. One pound of spices would have been sufficient for the complete burial process for any person. Josephus, an ancient Jewish historian of Jesus' time, told about a particularly loved, well-known, and wealthy priest who was buried with as much as 40 pounds of spices, a sign of the honor that was given to him in death. Read again that Nicodemus brought a gift of 100 pounds of spices, which equaled 10-12 gallons of wonderfully smelling oils. Such a gift indicated that Nicodemus was being overwhelmingly generous and that Jesus would be buried more like a king than a carpenter.

For Nicodemus to step out from his Pharisee community, one of the most vocal critics of Jesus and his followers, and assist with burying Jesus would have been quite a surprise. His actions show that he had respect for Jesus beyond what his community could keep him from showing. For Nicodemus to volunteer to handle Jesus' body in death was for him to take on the temporary title of "unclean," meaning he could not go back to his community, to the Temple, or do anything related to his calling or role. For him to honor Jesus as a king with such an overwhelming gift of burial oils shows that he truly recognized that Jesus was the long-awaited Messiah.

What images does the word *luxury* suggest? When have you experienced luxury?

How is honor shown today to people who have died? What do you think about these customs? Why?

Why do you think Nicodemus provided so lavishly for Jesus at his burial? What are some reasons for giving to this extreme? Which, if any, of those reasons might have applied to Nicodemus?

When have someone's actions surprised you? When has your willingness to accept a certain responsibility you and/or others?

Think of a time when someone vastly different from you, perhaps even a stranger, showed you honor and respect. For many, sadly, this may never happen. How did (would) such an outpouring affect you?

When have you faced the reality that serving God isn't easy? How did you handle that situation? How have you felt God's love and guidance during those times?

Think of a moment in your faith journey when you needed to act, but hesitated. What things held you back? What worries do you have that affect your judgment? How do the frustrations you face on your faith journey affect your ability to follow Jesus and be a faithful disciple?

Workers Ahead

We all like to receive gifts. While it is nice to honor someone in death, how much better to show your love and respect while they are living. One may wonder why Nicodemus chose to show his allegiance with Jesus at this point, when he had been hesitant to do so earlier.

In the beginning of our lives of discipleship, we, like Nicodemus, are full of questions and always ready to learn. However, as we mature into our faith, we may be more easily distracted. Perhaps what is most destructive to our spiritual lives is facing hardships and situations where being a disciple is extremely difficult. In such situations we are tempted not to finish our journey. We may get frustrated that being a disciple requires us to "get dirty" or do something that leaves blue lines on our ceilings. We may become angry that what God calls us to do isn't as easy as we would like for it to be.

In the Rear View

Let us draw strength from our friend Nicodemus. As a well-known Jew, a Pharisee, a greatly respected elder in his community, he had absolutely no business being at the blood-stained cross of Jesus. The Jewish people were either scared to support Jesus publicly, or their attitudes toward him had been soured by the Pharisees. The Pharisees were adamantly against Jesus. He had the gall to go against those things that they held most dear, to challenge their authority and the way they had interpreted God's teachings. The other elders and Jewish leaders had made up their minds regarding Jesus a long time before his death. Even though it was a long time coming, Nicodemus finally stood against the other religious leaders and showed his support to Jesus and approval of his teachings.

In your prayers today, ask that God to show you the path of being visibly faithful to your call. Almighty and gracious God, give us the confidence of Nicodemus so that we might be able to speak despite our positions, despite the religious expectations, despite what difficulties we may face on our journey, and you might be able to speak through us.

Travel Log

Day 1:

Think about a time of your spiritual journey that determined your future journey. Journal about that experience and how you knew God was on the journey with you.

Day 2:

List regular practices that might put you in a position to be able to hear what God is calling you to do. What steps are necessary to begin these practices? Make plans to start these practices.

Day 3:

Write a prayer that you can remember easily. Keep the prayer simple. When you are in "over your head," use it to calm yourself so that you can actually listen to God.

Day 4:

In your mind, sort through people you know but are not ones to whom you regularly give gifts. Choose one person and think about what that person really needs—not just a surface thing, but something that may mean sacrificial giving for you. Write a plan that will help you to provide this need for that person and work to make it happen. Nicodemus moved beyond the regular to give his gift to Jesus.

Day 5:

Write about the most extravagant gift you have ever received. How did that gift make you feel toward the giver? toward yourself? Record your thoughts.

Day 6:

Recently the tenor of society has been one of hate, exclusivity, and intolerance. People do not want to take up for the week against bullies, etc. Write a litany of unity to be used in your church's worship service. Ask your pastor to include it or to publish it in your church's newsletter.

Day 7:
Write down barriers and frustrations that block you from being the Christian God has called you to be. Write a prayer to God, lifting up Jesus, Nicodemus, and others as examples for you to follow.

Separation of Church and State

Scripture for lesson: Mark 15:37-39

Written by Steven Shelton

In my childhood, each Easter season was marked with the showing of the Charlton Heston film *The Ten Commandments*. Even today that world famous movie informs how many people view the ancient world, most specifically the biblical narrative surrounding Moses and the escape of God's people from Egypt. As Easter nears, I usually check to see when the movie will be broadcast so that I can watch at least a portion of it. Across the years, I've seen the movie at least a dozen times, but only once or twice all in one sitting.

Predating *The Ten Commandments* by three years was a lesser known (to modern audiences, at least) biblical epic film called *The Robe*, which starred Richard Burton, Jean Simmons, Victor Mature, and Michael Rennie. As a reference for the Generation X and Millennials out there, the biblical epic was to the 1950s what the superhero movie is to the 2010s. As with most of the films that fit into the biblical epic genre, *The Robe* was a grand spectacle, winning the Golden Globe for Best Picture and Academy Awards for Art Direction and Costume Design.

The film tells the story of a Roman military leader and his encounter with Jesus at the cross. His experience at the cross changes him, and the robe he wins as a result of casting lots next to the cross connects him to both his savior and to his destiny. While the movie is filled with the enormity of fully orchestrated musical background, sweeping landscapes, and complex and beautiful costumes, a great deal of screen time is spent explaining and deepening the complex relationship that the government of Rome had with the variety of local religions under its control. The climactic moment at the conclusion of the movie deals with the Roman emperor confronting the soldier, insisting that he renounce Jesus and recommit himself to Rome, thus maintaining his civic, financial, and spiritual loyalty to her. The soldier resisted and the final scenes of the movie show the soldier and his wife being taken away to be executed. (Their attempted execution and aftermath are the subject of *The Robe*'s sequel, *Demetrius and the Gladiators*.)

This relationship between faith and religion on one side and government and loyalty to the state on the other side becomes very complicated both in epic movies and in our personal lives. The film serves as a

What movies or other media have impacted your understanding of the biblical narrative?

reminder of the separation that exists for many of us and the difficulties we may face from time to time regarding how we live out our faith in places that are not friendly to religious talk.

The script writer took a single mention in the biblical narrative and turned it into a two and a half hour movie. I can't blame the writers and directors for imagining, though. For a military leader to confess publicly that Jesus truly was God's Son is surprising and inspiring.

Prep for the Journey

Ancient Rome was known for its highly organized and much disciplined military. A great many stories have passed into legend where relatively few Roman soldiers resolutely followed their brilliant commander and managed to overcome incredible odds. Throughout Rome's history, official tactics changed from time to time, but at the time of Jesus, the largest and most famous unit of the army was the legion, which was composed of the basic foot soldier of the army.

A legion was composed of approximately 5,000 men. Each legion was divided into 10 cohorts composed of roughly 500 men each, but with the first cohort having twice the number of soldiers. The generals of the legion typically traveled with the first cohort. Nine of the cohorts were divided into six centuries of about 80 men each, but the first cohort, the largest, consisted of five centuries of double the usual size, about 160 men each. Thus there were in all 59 centuries in a legion. The leader of each century was a centurion. The highest-ranking centurion was the leader of the first cohort.

The legion responsible for keeping the peace in Judea was probably divided between several cities in the area. Most likely, Jerusalem housed several centuries, or perhaps an entire cohort of soldiers. This century was tasked with overseeing the Roman executions of the day, which included Jesus and the two criminals crucified on either side of him. The soldiers would have arranged for the wood, the location, the physical labor of putting the men on the crosses, and ensuring that no one tried to rescue them. Because of the large following that Jesus had acquired and the notable parade when he entered the city a week earlier, the Romans were paying close attention to Jesus. To have a centurion and his company present at a crucifixion showed that the government was afraid there might be trouble from his followers. The taunts Jesus endured, "Save yourself!" show that his being rescued was on their minds and put them on watch. In fact, the selection of the hill of Golgotha as the place of Jesus' execution may have been in part military strategy as defending the top of a hill is tactically an easier task than a plain or a valley.

What is your opinion about troops sent to keep peace? How effective do you think military efforts can be in the effort to keep peace?

How do you feel about military strategy being part of the choice for Jesus' crucifixion site?

But it quickly became apparent that no one was coming to rescue Jesus. His followers were all gone. The centurion was not concerned with having to face a battle that day, so instead turned his attention to the man being executed. Something about the way Jesus was dying made an impression on the centurion. He was a man accustomed to watching the deaths of his enemies and of his fellow soldiers, but in Jesus' death, something made him recognize that Jesus was different and that the rumors were true. He really was God's son!

On the Road

Read Mark 15:37-39.

Then Jesus gave a loud cry and breathed his last. ³⁸ And the curtain of the temple was torn in two, from top to bottom. ³⁹ Now when the centurion, who stood facing him, saw that in this way he breathed his last, he said, "Truly this man was God's Son!"

After being hung on the cross, Jesus lived only six hours; the average time a person lived after being crucified was 12 hours, but some lingered even longer. Jesus cried out and died. Many scholars believe that this cry "was really 'a great shout'—not a cry of despair, or relief,… but the shout of a victor;…What impressed the centurion was the way Jesus died as a victor, a triumphant hero" (*The Interpreter's Bible, Vol. 7,* © 1951, page 907).

The centurion had an open mind and changed his opinion from believing that they were crucifying three criminals to understanding that Jesus was the son of God. The centurion "was deeply impressed no doubt by the courage of Jesus [and]…the convincing evidence of goodness and greatness. So he allowed the facts to shape a new judgment" (ibid).

For the centurion to have voiced his thoughts aloud is quite surprising. While the disciples should have been the voices at the foot of the cross, bearing witness to the divinity of Jesus, it was the centurion who gave voice to these truths. Making such a statement in front of the soldiers he commanded had the potential to disrupt to their militaristic cohesiveness. If the soldiers thought that their leader was beginning to believe in this mysterious Jewish man rather than the Roman Pantheon of Gods, their loyalty to him might have faltered, which would have spelled trouble in their next battle. The centurion could not help his proclamation. Anyone within reach of his voice heard his declaration.

What caused you to realize that Jesus is God's son?

While military history isn't a favorite subject for most people, in better understanding this nameless centurion, how has your opinion of him changed?

In the ongoing conflicts around the world related to religion and terrorism, what decisions might modern soldiers face? How might their faith influence those decisions?

How does hear a member of the armed forces attest to his or her faith in God, make you feel? Why?

How does a political candidate's claim of being a Christian influence you? Why? How does your faith influence your political decisions (like who you vote for)?

How effective do you think the United States is in separating church and state? What are some of the pros and cons of doing so?

How has the separation of church and state caused you a problem or provided safety for you?

What might be the equivalent of the Temple for you? your congregation?

At the time of this writing, the United States has just endured a brutal election season. It seems that the inauguration of our new president has not lessened the conflicts and arguments playing out in the news. In fact, I think the conflicts may even have gotten worse.

It's quite "cringe worthy" when a candidate for office attempts to connect with those with whom he or she has little in common. Making a speech to evangelical or mainline Christians and misquoting scripture or misusing common "church-speak" phrases just shows how unfamiliar that politician is with who we are and what we do.

In the United States, the government and religion are separate entities. The Constitution of the United States was written 300 years after the Spanish Inquisition, 300 years after the English debacle between Bloody Mary and Queen Elizabeth (a Protestant/Catholic conflict), 200 years after the French wars between Catholics and Protestants, 150 years after the 30 Years' War in Europe (also between the Catholics and Protestants), and a little more than 100 years after the War of the Three Kingdoms between England, Scotland, and Ireland, also related to the Church of England, Protestantism, and Catholicism. It's no surprise then, as the founding fathers started to write the Constitution, they were keenly aware of the religious wars that they had left behind in England and Europe.

A separation between the religion that a people follow and the government that leads and protects them was also a part of the success of Rome. As groups of people from various nations were assimilated, they were allowed to keep their religions, even as Rome levied heavy taxes on them and many of their men were drafted into the military. However, these men would often return home many years later with Roman citizenship, leading to an interesting plurality of loyalties both to Rome and to a local religion.

The Jewish people were no different in this regard. They were allowed to keep their religion and even their synagogues and the Temple in Jerusalem for their daily sacrifices and annual celebrations. It wasn't until the Jewish people rebelled several decades after Jesus' time that the Roman government punished them by destroying the Temple and much of the city. This Second Temple (the first belonging to Solomon) was never replaced, and many Jewish people today still long for the building of the Third Temple.

Workers Ahead

Our lives must reflect who we are as followers of Jesus, the Messiah. When it comes to the actions that might result from our identity as followers of Christ, many of those opportunities have been taken over by the very governmental forces from which we seek to be separate. During the past few hundred years, the church was always on the front lines of combating poverty, homelessness, and other societal concerns. The New Testament contains many injunctions to care for the "widows and orphans" among us. However, the church has gradually given up its place as the source of generosity, relying instead on the government and civic organizations. However, the government and civic organizations cannot meet all of the needs, nor would they share their faith with people.

Sometimes as we look at our roles in the church, we keep the separation between us and our government present in the roles we take. "Why do we need to help that poor, single mom? She gets a welfare check and food stamps. Why does that veteran need someone to check on her? The Veterans' Administration should be meeting her needs. Why does this homeless man need my support? Isn't there a city or state sponsored program that would help him to get job skills?"

God has called us to minister to people. Throughout history Christians have organized and opened hospitals, schools, orphanages, shelters, and so forth. Churches have begun to see that they should have continued their involvement. During the past dozen or so years, I've personally seen faithful congregations organize food pantries and clothes closets, feed and house people who are homeless, and offer special childcare days to give single parents time to run errands or just get a few hours of sleep.

The centurion shows us that despite our civic roles, our faith roles should never fade and never falter. God calls us to be present and to step forward—to speak, to act, to serve, and to love—especially when no one else will.

How do you feel about the church rather than the government/civic organizations taking responsibility for societal needs?

What needs in your community are not being met? How can your church minister to those people?

How often do your political opinions influence your spiritual decisions (like where you attend church)?

How might your faith influence your civic and political actions? How might we be able to allow the separation between government and religion that rightfully exists in our culture not to be present in our lives?

In the Rear View

Many leaders will say that having your faith as a central element of your political and civic life is necessary to maintain authentic leadership. However, the centurion forgot his separation and was able to see the truth about Jesus, despite his government role and his history.

Almighty and gracious God, Give us the wisdom of the centurion, that though our government might be free from religious influence, our souls are united with the Spirit of God, seeking to live a whole life, not one divided and separated. May your Spirit help us to be honestly, faithfully, and tactfully authentic in all aspects of our lives. May our voices shout your glory! Amen.

Travel Log

Day 1:

In today's society, many people, especially politicians, claim to be Christians while doing or saying things that are in direct opposition to Jesus' teachings. Look through a newspaper or Internet news and identify actions that proclaim to be Christian that you believe are counter to what the Bible teaches. Then look up scripture verses that support or deny what you believe. What surprises do you find?

Day 2:

Look up the law that talks about separation between church and state. Note the differences of what you might have heard people talk about and what it truly states.

Day 3:

Write a description of the scene of the Crucifixion complete with the other two people on the cross, the centurion, and the crowd or draw a picture of it. This might help you to put yourself in the scene and experience some of the feelings at the story evolves. What do you feel?

Day 4:

Journal about what you think was going through the centurion's mind that made him declare, "Truly this man was God's son!"

Day 5:

How do you feel about the separation of church and state? Record your thoughts on the subject.

Day 6:

Brainstorm a list of possible ministries that you and/or your church could do in place of the dwindling funds to help those who are poor.

Day 7:

Review the questions posed in the final section of this lesson ("In the Rear View"). Journal your thoughts/responses to these questions.

The Stones Will Cry Out

Scripture for lesson: Acts 2:1-4, 41-42, 6:1-5, 8-10; 7:51-53

Written by Chris Warren

As a teenager, I won an essay contest, which entitled me to a trip to Washington, D.C. The notification call came on Maundy Thursday as my family and I were preparing to go to church. The pastor had asked us to come in, take communion, and leave in complete silence. I remember my mother whispering the news to my aunt and grandmother before we entered the church; the news was simply too exciting not to share!

Stephen must have felt somewhat like my mother and I did when he was telling others about Jesus, the Christ. He refused to be silenced.

Prep for the Journey

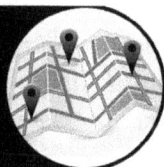

Some modern interpreters of the Bible are proponents of the "Prosperity Gospel." Many of you have probably heard preachers espouse this interpretation. It is often quite easy to find someone preaching this message simply by flipping through the channels on your television.

In a nutshell, the message of the prosperity gospel is that God wants you to be happy, and God will give you the material means to make you happy. If you can only have enough faith, only ask enough times, God will give you a house, a car, a fat wallet, and a sizable bank account. Many of these prosperity preachers can point to themselves as examples of how much money you can make by having faith in God.

This message ignores the truth that many of us have come to know, that happiness is not found in material things. But not only does this message ignore the source of true happiness, it also suggests that when people are being faithful to God they will be healthy, fulfilled, unconcerned about money or bills, and kept safe by God. In the Book of Acts we find examples of the extremely faithful who, despite their faith, suffered and were killed. Maybe faithfulness to God is

When have you refused to be silenced?

What kinds of things have you had to suffer for your faith? What kinds of sacrifices are you willing to make for the good of the church and in faithfulness to Christ? How might your answers to these questions have changed over time?

not such a guarantee of safety and comfort. Maybe it is dangerous to follow Christ.

On the Road

The previous lessons in this study have focused on little-known characters associated with Jesus' crucifixion and death and the importance of their roles. While seemingly most of Jesus' disciples deserted him during his time of greatest need, these few remained with him. It was as if they felt compelled to be there, risking society's stigma, the loss of careers, persecution, and a host of other things. After Jesus' resurrection and the coming of the Holy Spirit at Pentecost, the disciples and other followers began to share Jesus' teachings to all who would listen. One of those people was Stephen, who became the first Christian martyr.

Read Acts 2:1-4, 41-42.

When the day of Pentecost had come, they were all together in one place. ² And suddenly from heaven there came a sound like the rush of a violent wind, and it filled the entire house where they were sitting. 3 Divided tongues, as of fire, appeared among them, and a tongue rested on each of them. 4 All of them were filled with the Holy Spirit and began to speak in other languages, as the Spirit gave them ability.
...
So those who welcomed his message were baptized, and that day about three thousand persons were added. ⁴² They devoted themselves to the apostles' teaching and fellowship, to the breaking of bread and the prayers.

The day of Pentecost was an incredible time in the history of the church. It is the day Christians celebrate as the beginning of the church, and it was awesome. The Spirit filled the Apostles, and they preached to all the people who had gathered. Amazingly, people from all over the world heard the message in their native language. The power of God was shown to the people of Jerusalem that day. Then Peter spoke to the entire crowd and challenged them, telling them the story of Jesus' life, death, and resurrection. When he had finished speaking, those in the crowd asked what they needed to do to be saved. That day about 3000 people became believers in Jesus.

Such fast growth within the believers was awesome, but it caused several problems. Much like any organization, the church had some growing pains. Some were relatively trivial, but over time their conflicts with the ruling class of the Jewish people grew, and things became violent.

What have you felt compelled to do for Christ? the church? others? What did you risk in order to fulfill this call?

Who challenges you in regard to your spiritual life? How have you responded to those challenges?

What growing pains (or lack thereof) have affected your congregation? How has the congregation responded?

The accounts in the first several chapters of Acts are about conflicts between two different groups of Jewish people. When the author uses the phrase "the Jews" to talk about the enemies of the church, it indicates the members of the Jewish ruling class who were opposed to the way of Christ. There were some in that class, and obviously many other Jews, who accepted Jesus as the Messiah. As the commentary in the New Interpreter's Study Bible states, "Christians must clearly denounce all contemporary forms of Christian anti-Judaism as abhorrent." (page1971)

Factors that contributed to the conflicts between Jewish factions and between Gentile and Jewish groups within the church were the intense, quick growth of the church, the need for leadership to focus on evangelism rather than pastoral care, and the escalating attacks from the Jewish religious leaders who wanted to stop the church's momentum.

Read Acts 6:1-5, 8-10.

Now during those days, when the disciples were increasing in number, the Hellenists complained against the Hebrews because their widows were being neglected in the daily distribution of food. ² And the twelve called together the whole community of the disciples and said, "It is not right that we should neglect the word of God in order to wait on tables. ³ Therefore, friends, select from among yourselves seven men of good standing, full of the Spirit and of wisdom, whom we may appoint to this task, ⁴ while we, for our part, will devote ourselves to prayer and to serving the word." ⁵ What they said pleased the whole community, and they chose Stephen, a man full of faith and the Holy Spirit, together with Philip, Prochorus, Nicanor, Timon, Parmenas, and Nicolaus, a proselyte of Antioch.

…

⁸ Stephen, full of grace and power, did great wonders and signs among the people. ⁹ Then some of those who belonged to the synagogue of the Freedmen (as it was called), Cyrenians, Alexandrians, and others of those from Cilicia and Asia, stood up and argued with Stephen. ¹⁰ But they could not withstand the wisdom and the Spirit with which he spoke.

There was a conflict within the church about how the food was being distributed to the widows. The Greek-speaking Christians felt that their widows were being treated unfairly. Because the apostles were busy preaching and teaching, other followers were chosen to care for the believers and resolve disputes that arose. Stephen was one of those appointed to this important work.

Stephen was chosen from the entire group of followers, which numbered well over 3,000 people, as one who was trustworthy and faithful. God confirmed that faithfulness through Stephen's working of what scripture calls "great wonders and signs among the people." Within just a few verses, Stephen went from being a member of the church to a caretaker of the followers to a performer of wonders and signs.

What kind of changes might have to happen to the structure of your church if you had a one-day growth of 3000 people? What kinds of challenges might such growth bring? How might it cause conflict?

What do you perceive to be the differences between the Christian members of the Jewish faith and the Jewish religious leaders? Why was there such great conflict?

How does your congregation deal with conflict? How does it choose leaders?

What natural leaders have emerged in your congregation? How are you supporting and encouraging them?

What threat did Stephen represent to the Temple system?

Where do threats to systems of power exist today? How do those in power deal with those threats?

How have you been threatened by or represented a threat to someone's power in your life? What were the repercussions?

When have you either been purposely or mistakenly accused of actions counter to God? What was your defense? How did it feel to have to defend your actions?

The last designation is what ultimately caused the Jewish religious leaders to notice Stephen. It was obvious that God was working through Stephen in a mighty way, which gave additional credence to this new "sect" and threatened the authority of the traditional Jewish leaders. Stephen was questioned by people who had authority in the Temple system, arrested, and eventually taken before the council in what appears to be a cross between a legal court and a murderous mob. Stephen, chosen by the people as a faithful representative of God, given power by God to work wonders, was not rewarded in what we would consider to be earthly ways for his faithfulness. Instead, he was attacked and brutally killed.

Scenic Route

We might expect that when Stephen was arrested, he would have made a quick and clear defense of his actions. I can imagine myself in the situation saying something along the lines of, "Did you see those wonders and signs? Do you really think I am against God if God is working through me in that way?" Or maybe I would invoke the apostles, "You tried to keep them quiet, but you can surely see that what they are doing is wonderful. Do you really think they are enemies of God?"

But Stephen took a different tactic, one that was bolder than I think I would have dared to try. Stephen went back to the beginning of the Jewish faith. Starting with Abraham, Stephen argued that God's people had always rebelled against God. In 7:9 Stephen spoke about the jealousy of the patriarchs, the very people after whom the twelve tribes were named, and he showed how their lack of faithfulness to God caused the trials that Joseph experienced. These things even led to the enslavement of the people in Egypt.

Then Stephen implicated the people through the time of Moses, who was possibly the most revered figure in the history of Judaism. He was the people's leader, their savior from slavery and oppression. Within a few days of his absence, the people were creating idols of foreign gods to lead them in the wilderness, or perhaps back to Egypt. Jesus was like a modern Moses who did even more for the people, literally leading them out of slavery, but freeing them from slavery to sin. Still the people rejected Jesus. Stephen concluded with the following statement:

Read Acts 7:51-53.

"You stiff-necked people, uncircumcised in heart and ears, you are forever opposing the Holy Spirit, just as your ancestors used to do. [52]

Which of the prophets did your ancestors not persecute? They killed those who foretold the coming of the Righteous One, and now you have become his betrayers and murderers. ⁵³ You are the ones that received the law as ordained by angels, and yet you have not kept it."

Notice that Luke (the author of Acts) writes about Stephen in ways that help us to connect him with Jesus, and in some ways with Moses. In 6:15, Luke writes, "...all who sat in the council looked intently at him, and they saw that his face was like the face of an angel." This verse may remind us of how Moses' faced glowed after he had been in God's presence. Perhaps it reminds us of how Jesus' face shone like the sun at the Transfiguration.

As Stephen's end was about to come, Luke said that Stephen saw a vision. Acts 7:56 quotes Stephen, "Look...I see the heavens opened and the Son of Man standing at the right hand of God!" In that moment the people seized him to take him outside the city to stone him. This verse might remind us of the opening of heaven when Jesus was baptized.

Perhaps the greatest allusion to Stephen being like Jesus, amidst the working of wonders, the great faithfulness he showed, his face being like an angel's, and his vision of heaven is the recording of Stephen's last words. As he was being stoned to death, Stephen says in verse 59, "Lord Jesus, receive my spirit." And then as he was breathing his last, he cried out in verse 60, "Lord, do not hold this sin against them." These words are clear references to Jesus' words from the cross as he was being crucified.

Workers Ahead

We have learned something from the life of Stephen. God calls us to apply that learning to what we do every day. I imagine that we all see something different and meaningful from Stephen's story that we can apply to our own lives.

We started this lesson talking about the "prosperity gospel," which claims that God rewards the faithful with wealth, comfort, and good health. Stephen obviously did not experience these rewards. He, of course, received an eternal reward, but not the type of earthly wealth about which such preachers.

One thing we might learn from Stephen's story is that God's rewards for faithfulness are not always clearly perceivable in our own lifetimes. The ways in which people might be rewarded for faithfulness are much more complicated than the simple message that if you have enough faith, God will fill your bank account.

Another way we can apply Stephen's story to our own lives is to be

---

If you were Stephen and had said these words in this situation, what would you have expected top happen?

What does it mean to be faithful in the face of powerful opposition in today's world?

What does the author want to convey to the reader by making such references to Jesus' life? What do you make of these references about Stephen?

Whom do you know who resembles Christ? In what ways do you see Christ in this person?

What have you learned from Stephen's life? How will you apply it to your daily life?

What rewards have you experienced as a result of living faithfully?

How have you testified to the love and power of Christ in your life? How can you share that faith with others?

When have you remained faithful to God despite extreme circumstances? What enabled you to do so?

How can you increase your faithfulness to God?

willing to testify to our relationship with Christ, even when we are in adverse circumstances. His testimony of Christ's love revealed in the world is powerful and one that we should always be ready to share. A part of that sharing should also include how Christ's love has changed us and what gives us the faith to trust in Jesus.

In the Rear View

Pentecost was a wonderful day in the life of the church, but soon thereafter the great growth that began at Pentecost caused some problems for the apostles and for the new community. As a remedy to some of those problems, the church appointed some people from within the church to oversee day-to-day issues. Stephen was one of the appointees, but he didn't only deal with the issue of how food distribution. He also preached about Jesus, causing the people who liked the current power structure to become nervous.

Once brought before the council, Stephen didn't back down, but instead charged his accusers of being unfaithful to God themselves. Stephen remained faithful to God, and he paid for doing so with his life.

In our modern world faithfulness to God has sometimes come to mean that we don't have to make any sacrifices; to some people it has come to mean that God will reward them with earthly things because they believe. These interpretations are not scriptural, and they are affecting the integrity of the Christian Church. Jesus, the greatest example of faithfulness, was not rewarded in earthly ways for his faithfulness, and those who walk in his footsteps should expect to be either. But being faithful to God is not about rewards, but about serving the Master of the Universe.

Travel Log

Day 1:

Take a moment to reflect on someone in your life who has been faithful to God. What kind of impact has he or she had on you? Take a moment to write about this person in the space below. How do you see faithfulness to God in his or her life? Where do you see sacrifice in this person's life? In what ways would you like to be more like that person?

Day 2:

When the day of Pentecost came, the disciples were all together, and the Spirit moved within them. Take a moment to breathe and try to remove distractions. Focus on the Holy Spirit. Invite the Spirit to be with you and to move within you. Be patient. You may experience a revelation, and you may not. You may even want to make this type of time in the Spirit a daily practice.

Take a moment and write down what this time in the Spirit was like for you. How can you invite the Spirit deeper into your life?

Day 3:

Many times in the story of Stephen, Luke used words and images that connected Stephen to Christ. He spoke of his appearance and even quoted the same words that Jesus used on the cross.

What in the lives of people you know or in your own life resembles Christ? As Christians, we are called to walk in Christ's footsteps. Doing so will likely give us opportunities to resemble Christ just a little. Think or write about ways that you can follow Christ more closely so that you may resemble him more.

Day 4:

Most of us will not be called to make the types of sacrifices that Stephen did, but we are still called to sacrifice ourselves for the sake of the gospel.

Make a list of ways that you are sacrificing for the sake of the gospel right now. What are some other things for which you are sacrificing? Make a list of those, too. Be as honest as you can. Take a few moments to ponder the balance in your lists and in your life.

Day 5:

Many of us deal with power struggles in our schools, our work, and other parts of our lives. We certainly see these kinds of struggles in the world of politics. Where have you seen people forcibly quieted because their ideas or desires represented a threat to the status quo? Write down some examples below, and try to include ways of responding to people's desire for power, even at the cost of truth.

Day 6:

Stephen's speech to the Temple authorities brings up ways that Christians in every age should converse with people of other faiths. As stated in the lesson, the argument that led to Stephen's death was among people of the same faith who differed about Jesus. Eventually these two branches separated, but at the time of Stephen's death, they had not yet done so.

Some have used Stephen's speech and other writings in the New Testament to justify hateful speech and actions against those of other faiths, but such actions are against Jesus' message for the church.

Take a moment to write down instances where persons of a particular faith have been disrespectful to those of another tradition. Maybe someone was disrespectful to Christians, maybe a Christian was disrespectful to someone else. How should such a situation be handled? How would Jesus respond? How should the faith community respond when one of its members has been disrespectful of the faith of others?

Day 7:

Think about the idea of a prosperity gospel. What are you working toward in this life? Does something within you say that if God really loved you, you would receive those things?

It may be easy to set aside those notions about money, but what about health? Do we not sometimes think that if God really loved us, God would take away our pain, our disease, our mental illness?

Write down some things that you wish you had in your life. How hard are you working to get those things? Now write down the things that are missing in your relationship with God. Maybe prayer time, offering of time or gifts or money, something else. How hard are you working to achieve those goals?